A Gentle Walk

A QUARTERLY FAITH JOURNAL

Cathy Tooley

Copyright © 2025 by Cathy Tooley

All rights reserved. This book may not be reproduced or stored in whole or in part by any means without the written permission of the author except for brief quotations for the purpose of review.

ISBN: 978-1-966343-29-5 (soft cover)

Edited by: Amy Ashby

Published by Warren Publishing
Charlotte, NC
www.warrenpublishing.net
Printed in the United States

Let's Walk Together

Ready to craft a resolution toward growing your relationship with God that truly reflects your current behaviors? Look no further than this journal. Divided into four quarters, this journal offers ample space for reflection and growth.

You can start your journey any month, or any day, and track your progress and how you evolve in your faith over the proceding twelve months. As the saying goes, it's a journey and the most important thing is that you are on the path.

With Bible verses for reflection prompts and journal entries for each day of the month, you can track your progress and revisit insights, "aha" moments, and key questions from your spiritual journey at the start of each new quarter. Take time to reflect on your journey, noting areas of growth and opportunities for improvement on the provided action plan pages.

As you delve into Quarter 4's reflective questions, mark those that inspire goals for the upcoming year. This journal will become a roadmap for your spiritual journey with God, guiding you toward self-improvement, fulfillment, and a closer relationship to God as you invite Him into each and every day.

May God bless you on your journaling journey!

Happy journaling!

Welcome to Your Faith-Based Journal

We're so glad you're here.

Too often, Bible studies focus solely on taking in information. This journal invites you to go deeper—to engage with God's Word, reflect on meaningful prompts, journal your thoughts, and witness your spiritual growth over the course of a year.

WHAT TO EXPECT

Each day, you'll:
1. Read a question prompt
2. Read the corresponding Bible verse
3. Reflect on where you are today
   - What thoughts come to mind?
   - How does this prompt move your heart today?
   - What do you hear God speaking through His Word?

Write freely. Capture your thoughts, emotions, questions, and prayers. This journal is your space to connect with God intentionally and honestly.

HOW TO USE THIS JOURNAL

1. Start today. Open to the day of the month that you are starting (what is today's date?).
2. Read the verse and prompt. Let God's Word guide your heart.
3. Journal freely. Write your thoughts, prayers, and insights.
4. Reflect quarterly. Revisit your earlier entries and use the guided questions to explore your growth.
5. Repeat the cycle. As you return to Day 1 each quarter, notice what's shifted and celebrate the work God is doing in your life.

A JOURNEY THROUGH THE YEAR

The journal is divided into four quarters but don't worry about starting at the "right" time. You can begin whenever you're ready—what matters most is that you start. Your year-long journey begins the day you do.

REVISIT, REFLECT, AND GROW

At the beginning of each new quarter, return to Day 1. Read the same verse and prompt, but this time, revisit what you wrote three months ago. Then journal your new reflections.

Ask yourself:
- What has changed?
- How have I grown?
- What has God been teaching me?
- Where am I now in my faith journey?

Over time, you'll begin to see the threads of God's faithfulness and your transformation woven throughout the pages.

QUARTERLY ACTION PLANNING

At the end of each quarter, use the Action Plan pages to pause and pray about your next steps. Reflect on:
- What themes or patterns have emerged?
- What growth has taken place?
- What areas need healing, change, or deeper focus?
- What intentional steps will you take to walk more closely with God?

Over the next year, this journal will become a personal record of your spiritual journey—one filled with growth, challenges, transformations, and a deeper intimacy with God. May it be a sacred companion as you seek His presence, listen for His voice, and walk boldly in the purpose He has for you.

Are you ready to begin?

Day One

John 18:31-32

In a world where we are bombarded with images, sounds and impressions of who we are, who we are supposed to be, and what we are to follow, the only question should be:

Who is discipling YOU?

Quarter One

Quarter Two

Quarter Three

Quarter Four

Day Two

Romans 13:1-3

In a world that is forever political, "politics" are part of our culture. How do we avoid these distractions and temptations? Politics will stop being our demons when politicians stop being our gods.

How do politics show up as "demons" in your life? What can you do to change that?

Quarter One

Quarter Two

Quarter Three

Quarter Four

Day Three

1 Thessalonians 5:16-18, Psalms 103:1-4

Gratitude is a daily prayer of thanks for all that we have been given. Gratitude all in itself is a prayer.

What if you wake up tomorrow and all you have left is what you thanked God for yesterday? What are you thankful for from yesterday?

Quarter One

Quarter Two

Quarter Three

Quarter Four

Day Four

Acts 11:26, Acts 26:28

How we show up to people every day says more about our faith than anything we "say" about our faith.

If you were arrested for being a Christian would there be enough evidence to convict you?

What evidence did you display today?

Quarter One

Quarter Two

Quarter Three

Quarter Four

Day
Five

1Peter 10–11

God gives each of us unique and special gifts. These gifts are not like those of your neighbors, your friends, your siblings, your spouse, or anyone else; they are uniquely YOURS.

How can you give someone else what God gave only you to use for Him? What gifts did He give you, and how are you using them for Him?

Quarter One

Quarter Two

Quarter Three

Quarter Four

Day
Six

Jeremiah 31:34

God grants us so much grace. He promised that he does not "keep record" of our sins. Thank goodness!

If God kept a record of sins, who could stand? What sins are you still holding on to that you need to let go and let God?

Quarter One

Quarter Two

Quarter Three

Quarter Four

Day
Seven

Isaiah 48:10

God created us. He formed and made us to be His. Far too often we define the beginning and the ending of our stories instead of letting our Creator finish His Own work.

What if you have put a period where God intended a comma? What story is He still writing in your life that needs a comma rather than the period that *you* placed there?

Quarter One

_____
_____
_____

Quarter Two

_____
_____
_____

Quarter Three

_____
_____
_____

Quarter Four

_____
_____
_____

Day
Eight

*Romans 8:31,
Jeremiah 29:11*

God has plans for us always. And He is clear in His desires for goodness in our lives. He is also clear regarding what plans and actions He does not want in our lives.

Do you think a loving God would celebrate what He told you not to do? What do you need to let go of today? What things have you done that you need to lay at His feet?

Quarter One

Quarter Two

Quarter Three

Quarter Four

Day Nine

Romans 5:8, Psalm 36:7

Can you imagine looking at yourself through God's eyes? What would that be like?

What would I see if God gave me the gift of seeing what I can't see? Describe how God sees you.

Quarter One

Quarter Two

Quarter Three

Quarter Four

Day
Ten

Isiah 45:11

It is so easy to get caught up in what I *want* in my life rather than what God wants to *give* me.

Are your prayers a "see me" or a "give me"? Make a list of your regular prayers and label them "give me" or "see me." What do you notice?

Quarter One

Quarter Two

Quarter Three

Quarter Four

Day Eleven

I John 2:6, I Corinthians 11

Every single day you walk through your steps playing the "game" of life through your work, your relationships, your attitudes, your actions, and your words.

Does your game look anything like Jesus' game? In what ways is it similar, and in what ways is it different?

Quarter One

Quarter Two

Quarter Three

Quarter Four

Day
Twelve

Luke 8:18

From our first breath to our last, we know that Jesus has promised to come back. We get so busy "living" that we often do not focus on His promise.

If you knew Jesus were coming tomorrow, what would today look like? How would you spend your time? How would you spend your money? Who would you connect with? What would you do?

Quarter One

Quarter Two

Quarter Three

Quarter Four

Day
Thirteen

Romans 8:38-39, Psalms 139:7-9

Sometimes it can feel as if we are so isolated and alone in our lives —that somehow, someway God has forgotten us.

If you don't feel close to God, who moved?
What steps can you take to get closer to Him today?

Quarter One

Quarter Two

Quarter Three

Quarter Four

Day
Fourteen

John 12:42-43

In a world of influencers, social media hype, TV distortion, and false gods all around us, it is easy to get lost in likes, shares, follows, and subscribes.

Do you love the praise of man more than the praise of God? How are you seeking God's love over man's attentions?

Quarter One

Quarter Two

Quarter Three

Quarter Four

Day Fifteen

John 3:29-30

In the me, me, me world that we are living, sometimes it is so difficult to separate the line of increasing ME or increasing God.

Ask yourself, "Am I doing what I am doing to increase me or increase Him?" How so?

Quarter One

Quarter Two

Quarter Three

Quarter Four

Day
Sixteen

I Samuel 12:23

Sometimes it is so easy to blame someone else for what is happening in the world right now. The hatred, the divisiveness, the bitterness, and the pain all seem to be so prevalent all around us.

What if the issue is not the weakness of the world but rather the prayerlessness of the church? How can you start to change that? What is your prayer today?

Quarter One

Quarter Two

Quarter Three

Quarter Four

Day
Seventeen

Romans 8:18-30

In a world that is so thirsty for truth, light, justice, and love, you need to know that you can be that light.

Looking at those who are suffering ... what are they thirsty for? How can you help quench their thirst and be their light?

Quarter One

Quarter Two

Quarter Three

Quarter Four

Day Eighteen

James 5:9, Ephesians 4:26

It is so easy to keep track of those who have hurt us, isn't it? I'll bet there is a list (or at least a few names) that came to mind as you read that statement.

Aren't you glad Jesus gave up "paybacks" for you? Who do you need to forgive and let go of that "payback"?

Quarter One

Quarter Two

Quarter Three

Quarter Four

Day Nineteen

*Psalm 139:23-24,
Matthew 9:37-38*

It can seem like life is just moving right by us. Sometimes it's like we're riding in a car, looking out the window, watching images pass by.

Have we lost His way? How is God calling you to live your daily life? What are you doing/not doing that needs to change to move closer to Him?

Quarter One

Quarter Two

Quarter Three

Quarter Four

Day
Twenty

Hebrews 4:16

We all have wants and desires in our hearts.
We all have things that we ask God for.
You know, those big dreams, big plans, big prayers.

What are you praying for now that only God can do?
Ask God for the ONE thing, that big prayer,
that only He can bring you.

Quarter One

_____
_____
_____
_____

Quarter Two

_____
_____
_____
_____

Quarter Three

_____
_____
_____
_____

Quarter Four

_____
_____
_____
_____

Day
Twenty-one

James 1:17–18

The Father of Light and the father of darkness ARE with us every day. They surround our lives, our families, and the things that matter to us.

Which father do you resemble most often? The Father of Light or the father of darkness? How does your life epitomize the Father of Light? And what do you do daily to defeat the father of darkness?

Quarter One

Quarter Two

Quarter Three

Quarter Four

Day
Twenty-two

Psalms 34:17, Hebrews 4:15-16

There are times in our lives, situations in our lives, and pains in our lives that leave us feeling broken.

Where is there brokenness in you that must be healed? What is the brokenness in your life that you need God to heal? Search your heart and ask Him for healing.

Quarter One

Quarter Two

Quarter Three

Quarter Four

Day
Twenty-three

I Corinthians 7:17

If someone passed you on the street, what would they say about you? What would your family say about you and your faith? What would those you work with say about how much you love Jesus? What would your children, your spouse, your friends say about how you follow Jesus?

What would those who love you say about your faith? Would they know you love Jesus and live to follow Him? What would that "evidence" be?

Quarter One

Quarter Two

Quarter Three

Quarter Four

Day
Twenty-four

Psalms 63:1, Matthew 6:33

We give our real time and attention to the things that really matter to us. We are intimate and love the priorities in our lives. There is no fight worth winning if it costs you intimacy with God.

How are you becoming more intimate with God every day?

Quarter One

Quarter Two

Quarter Three

Quarter Four

Day
Twenty-five

Ephesians 4:15–16

Christianity is a TEAM sport. The Bible doesn't say you should only experience Jesus alone. He says you are to have a shared experience, be a part of the Body of Christ.

How are you building a "team" for Christ?

Quarter One

Quarter Two

Quarter Three

Quarter Four

Day
Twenty-six

*Philippians 4:13,
Exodus 15:2*

If you go through life without God's power, it is tragic. To never live the life He designed you for is a loss.

How can you seek and find the power God is calling in your life today? What does that look like?

Quarter One

Quarter Two

Quarter Three

Quarter Four

Day
Twenty-seven

Jeremiah 30:17

Judgment is a verb. We do it every day. We judge what people wear, what they say, the company they keep, what they do for a living, and the list goes on and on. But God's judgment is about healing and restoration. Who needs healing in your life? Maybe it's you? Maybe it's a loved one? Write down the names on your heart.

How can we judge like God? How can we begin to judge for healing and restoration?
Who do we need to judge for healing and restoration?

Quarter One

Quarter Two

Quarter Three

Quarter Four

Day
Twenty-eight

Philippians 1:21

In a YOLO world where we are far too often living only for ourselves, it is often difficult to remember the real purpose our lives were created for. Without Jesus, we live for ourselves; with Jesus, we live for those around us.

How are you living for "self," and how are you living for those around us?

Quarter One

Quarter Two

Quarter Three

Quarter Four

Day
Twenty-nine

*Ephesians 2:10,
Philippians 2:13*

We are masterfully and wonderfully made. God is such an amazing artist, and we are His handiwork. First God works ON us, then He works IN us, then he works THROUGH us.

How is God working on, in, and through you this quarter? Which one is strongest right now?

Quarter One

Quarter Two

Quarter Three

Quarter Four

Day Thirty

2 Timothy 3:16-17

You are chosen. You are special. You are God-made and scripture is God-breathed. Each and every part of you is HIS and made in His image. Regardless of what you see in that the mirror or what the world tells you, you are HIS.

What are you seeing today that makes it tough for you to believe that? How could you begin to see those things differently?

Quarter One

Quarter Two

Quarter Three

Quarter Four

Day Thirty-one

Proverbs 11:2

Pride is a tough trait to keep in check. We are proud of many things in our lives. But when we puff up with pride, we make it all about us rather than the submission to God and what He wants us to be.

Where in your life is God calling you to keep your pride in "check"? List those areas.

Quarter One

Quarter Two

Quarter Three

Quarter Four

Day
Thirty-two

I John 5:14–15

Has there ever been a time in your life when you felt as if your prayers were not answered? God tells us that our prayers will be answered when they are in alignment with the will of God in our lives. That can be a difficult pill to swallow.

Where are your prayers not seeming to be answered? What alignment adjustment might you need to make?

Quarter One

Quarter Two

Quarter Three

Quarter Four

Day Thirty-three

Moses 4: 3-4

We are not always taught how present Satan is in our lives and in the lives of those we love. We can easily forget that Satan's desires in our lives are not for good, but to steal, kill, and destroy. But the good news is that Satan is shrewd but not innovative; it's the same old tricks with him.

How have you seen Satan's lack of innovation show up in your life? Tell the story to remember his shrewdness but lack of innovation. This reminder will help you identify and protect yourself from his tactics.

Quarter One

Quarter Two

Quarter Three

Quarter Four

Day
Thirty-four

Proverbs 4:23

Our thoughts are like information put into a hard drive of a computer. They can either make the computer flow effortlessly and function in high capacity, or they can infect the computer and cause it to malfunction. The same is true with our thoughts. Are you allowing the thoughts God gives you to flow effortlessly?

What are the thoughts that God has given you about your life? Write them down and then invite the Holy Spirit to help God's words flow effortlessly and help you do His Will at a high capacity.

Quarter One

Quarter Two

Quarter Three

Quarter Four

Day
Thirty-five

Philippians 2:3

Have you ever thought to yourself, "They are so full of themselves." There is an old expression that when we recognize (and often don't like) a characteristic in others, it is because that characteristic really lives in us. *Ouch*. Christ sends no one away empty except for those who choose to be full of *themselves*. Is that you?

How might you be showing up to others as "full of yourself"? How can God help you adjust that?

Quarter One

_____
_____
_____
_____

Quarter Two

_____
_____
_____
_____

Quarter Three

_____
_____
_____
_____

Quarter Four

_____
_____
_____
_____

Day Thirty-six

Psalms 89:14, John 5:30

We are hardwired to judge. We have opinions about everything and, sadly, everyone. We far too often share those judgments—whether they are founded or not and without considering if they are helpful or not—especially when they are hidden behind a screen or a keyboard. Entrust yourself to the One who judges justly.

How are you judging others? Is it helpful or hurtful? How can you call on God to help you in this area?

Quarter One

Quarter Two

Quarter Three

Quarter Four

Day
Thirty-seven

1 John 5:4

Our lives in Christ begin and end with Jesus. Our faith is built on a virgin's womb and an empty tomb.

How are you living out that faith? How are you sharing that faith with others? What is one thing you can do today to share your faith with others?

Quarter One

Quarter Two

Quarter Three

Quarter Four

Day
Thirty-eight

Titus 3:7–8

Nobody gets me. No one knows me. No one really understands what I have been through or who I am. I know that nobody understands me like Jesus. In Him and only Him can I be known.

What does Jesus know about you that no one else does? Where and in what part of your life do you trust the One who knows you best—Jesus?

Quarter One

Quarter Two

Quarter Three

Quarter Four

Day
Thirty-nine

Hebrew 4:26

How are you praying? I mean really, what and how are you praying? God calls us to pray with divine assistance.

How can you pray today with divine assistance? What are your divine-assisted prayers? Invite the Holy Spirit to pray with you today. Write down your prayer for the Holy Spirit's divine assistance.

Quarter Two

Quarter Three

Quarter Four

Day Forty

Corinthians 13:12

In the "information highway" in which we all live, it is so easy to get overwhelmed with the images we see. Our brains often cannot process them all. But what if you let the way you love God impact how you process/take in information?

What are the items on your "information highway" that need to be filtered through God first?

Quarter One

Quarter Two

Quarter Three

Quarter Four

Day
Forty-one

Ecclesiastes 3:1

Patience is not my virtue. Ever said that? I know I have. Waiting is not my strong suit, and I'll bet that, depending on the situation, it is not yours either. What I have learned is that God's timing is not about what you see, it's about what you *don't* see.

How is God calling you to be patient in your current "ask"? How can you embrace this divinely appointed waiver?

Quarter One

_____

_____

_____

Quarter Two

_____

_____

_____

Quarter Three

_____

_____

_____

Quarter Four

_____

_____

_____

Day
Forty-two

Psalms 22:3

Does it ever seem like everyone else has a "better" relationship with Jesus than you do? Maybe it seems to you like they pray better, have more guidance, get more out of their prayers, and just, overall seem to have a more "direct line" to talk to Jesus. This I know for certain: Jesus goes where He is welcomed.

How are you welcoming Jesus into your life? What does that look like yesterday, today, and tomorrow? How will you make Him feel more welcomed in your life?

Quarter One

Quarter Two

Quarter Three

Quarter Four

Day
Forty-three

I Peter 2:9–10

As a Christian, you are called to be different. We are called to walk, talk, and behave differently. When Christians stop being different—the way we live, the way we parent, the way we act in our marriages and relationships, the way we spend our money, the way we think, and what we do with our time—our message stops being different.

How are you showing up as a Christian in your marriage and relationships, in the way you spend money, in the way you think, and in how you spend your time? Are you doing these things as Jesus has called you to?

Quarter One

Quarter Two

Quarter Three

Quarter Four

Day
Forty-four

John 3:16–17

God gave His only son to save you!
God doesn't "partially" save. He saves all of you.

How has God fully saved you?

Quarter One

Quarter Two

Quarter Three

Quarter Four

Day
Forty-five

Isaiah 48:10

Everything that has happened to you is your testimony.
From tears to tribulations. From the pain to your purpose.
From the hurt to the healing. He uses it all.
Your story is not about you. It is all about God.

What is your "story" that glorifies God?
How will you share that testimony with others?

Quarter One

Quarter Two

Quarter Three

Quarter Four

Day
Forty-six

Romans 12:19–21

Every day we get up. We brush our teeth, we make coffee, and we get ready for the day. Then we are off to continue our daily routines. And days turn into weeks, and weeks turn into months, and months turn into years. While we spend time looking at the micro, God is looking at the macro.

What is the macro you can see in your life? How can you use your daily micros to magnify that macro?

Quarter One

Quarter Two

Quarter Three

Quarter Four

Day
Forty-seven

John 17:3

Sometimes—well, sometimes too often—we think that if we ask, we will receive. You know, like going to a restaurant. You place your order, and you get what you ordered. God is not a transactional God; He is a relationship God. And you don't have a relationship with that restaurant, nor would you want one. We must first seek a *relationship* with God.

How are you seeking a relationship with God? Where are you thinking of God as "transactional"? How can you change that?

Quarter One

Quarter Two

Quarter Three

Quarter Four

Day Forty-eight

Exodus 13:17–18

Sometimes God takes us home the long way—
even when we don't like the path, or the path is hard,
or the path is unpleasant. Sometimes the hard way is the
only way to reach the promised land.

What is the "long" path God has you on right now
to reach your promised land? Write down the glimpses
of the promised land you can already see.

Quarter One

Quarter Two

Quarter Three

Quarter Four

Day
Forty-nine

Romans 12:2

In a divisive culture, where we are constantly pointing fingers at one another and the media is constantly polarizing and politicizing everything, it is so hard to see the forest for the trees sometimes.
But God calls us to follow His ways in our lives.

Is your identity shaped by scripture or by culture? How is culture shaping your life? How is scripture shaping your life? What changes do you need to make?

Quarter One

Quarter Two

Quarter Three

Quarter Four

Day Fifty

Matthew 24: 10-20

Have you ever heard the old expression, "Sometimes it gets worse before it gets better"? Take, for example, that day after surgery before you really begin healing. Or that tough breakup that leads to a new relationship for the better. Or the time you were fired but then found a job you love. Sometimes when we choose to follow God, it feels like things get worse before they get better.

Where are you on that journey now? Are things bad or getting better? What prayer can you ask of God to meet you where you are in that journey?

Quarter One

Quarter Two

Quarter Three

Quarter Four

Day
Fifty-one

John 10:7-9

A relationship with Jesus inspires a longing for others to know Him too. While it's natural to think that children raised in faith will follow Jesus, that is not always the case. The Lord urges us not to lose hope. Continue to be a faithful witness and take advantage of every opportunity to share your faith with your family and loved ones. The Lord tells us not to give up on our families knowing Christ. Maintain your witness and seize the opportunities when they come to witness.

How is your life a "witness" to those you love?
How can you be even more of a "witness"?

Quarter One

_____
_____
_____
_____

Quarter Two

_____
_____
_____
_____

Quarter Three

_____
_____
_____
_____

Quarter Four

_____
_____
_____
_____

Day
Fifty-two

John 14:15–24

Can you imagine a world where the commandments were a way of being? Not some old tablet containing lofty ideals, but actual reality. Can you imagine that?

How are you bringing the commandments to your life? How can you be a testimony to God's commandments?

Quarter One

Quarter Two

Quarter Three

Quarter Four

Day
Fifty-three

Exodus 20:3-6, I John 5:21

We are creatures of habit. We like what we like, and we do what we do out of comfort—especially when we are stressed. When we are stressed, we return to our old gods that are more comfortable.

What "gods" do you turn to in times of stress? How could God be your new sanctuary in stressful times?

Quarter One

Quarter Two

Quarter Three

Quarter Four

Day
Fifty-four

I Chronicles 16:34, I Thessalonians 5:18

Think about your life. What matters most: what people have done FOR you or who they ARE to you? Mature worship moves beyond what He has done for me to who He is to me.

Who is God to you? Is that the relationship you are wanting? How can you grow that?

Quarter One

Quarter Two

Quarter Three

Quarter Four

Day
Fifty-five

Matthew 17:20,
Romans 10:8–11

If you depend on always "feeling" God,
then you will feel alone. You must rely on faith.

How are you relying on faith today?

Quarter One

Quarter Two

Quarter Three

Quarter Four

Day
Fifty-six

Proverbs 11:2

Pride. There is so much power in that word. Pride is putting ourselves in a position other than where God has put us. *Ouch*.

Where has your pride put you that God did not put you? Ask God to move you into the position HE has for you.

Quarter One

Quarter Two

Quarter Three

Quarter Four

Day
Fifty-seven

Psalms 145: 8-9

Has anyone ever told you that you have a short fuse?
Don't worry; you're not the only one.

God is slow to anger, so should we be.
God is rich in love, so should we be.

How can you be slower to anger and quicker to love?
Where is God calling you to do just that? And, with whom?

Quarter One

Quarter Two

Quarter Three

Quarter Four

Day
Fifty-eight

John 8:11

What is right? What is wrong? And who gets to be the judge? Jesus loved sinners, but he did not endorse sin. If Jesus loved sinners, shouldn't we?

How can you love the sinner
but not endorse the sin today?

Quarter One

Quarter Two

Quarter Three

Quarter Four

Day
Fifty-nine

Romans 8: 28-39

Do you ever get exhausted in the planning, the organizing, the thinking, the hoping for things to turn out the way you want? Today I want to remind you that God tells us that *He* is behind the scenes mastering everything.

What can you stop controlling today since God is already behind the scenes mastering it anyway?

Quarter One

Quarter Two

Quarter Three

Quarter Four

Day Sixty

Isaiah 55:8-9

Sometimes life can have us praying a "let's make a deal" with God. "God, you give me this, and I will do that." Sound familiar?

How are you praying in a "let's make a deal" way to God? How can prayer look different today?

Quarter One

Quarter Two

Quarter Three

Quarter Four

Day
Sixty-one

1 Thessalonians 3

Everything you encounter, everything you go through, every joy and every pain is meant for purpose. Your life is a testimony of who Jesus is and what He has done.

What is your testimony this quarter?
Write down how Jesus has shown up for you.

Quarter One

Quarter Two

Quarter Three

Quarter Four

Day
Sixty-two

Psalm 139:16

Before you were even born, Jesus knew and loved you.
Jesus is there for you today, tomorrow, and in between.

What do you need to let Jesus have today to
make an even greater tomorrow?

Quarter One

Quarter Two

Quarter Three

Quarter Four

Day
Sixty-three

I John 2:6

We are called to follow in His steps. Sometimes, in my journey with God, He changes direction, and I must adapt and move with Him. Sometimes He moves, and I need to move with Him.

How are you following in God's steps today? Where is He calling you to move, yet you are still standing still?

Quarter One

Quarter Two

Quarter Three

Quarter Four

Day
Sixty-four

Matthew 17:5

The Father calls us to submit to Jesus. To follow Jesus. When Jesus calls … you come!

Where is Jesus calling you to go? What is He calling you to say? How is He calling you to submit?

Quarter One

Quarter Two

Quarter Three

Quarter Four

Day Sixty-five

John 12:28,
I Corinthians 10:31

To some He has given many, and to all He has given some.
God wants us to use whatever we have for His glory...
He gave it to us anyway.

What did God give you—what talents, what gifts,
what treasures? How are you using it for His glory?

Quarter One

Quarter Two

Quarter Three

Quarter Four

Day
Sixty-six

Acts 3:16, Deuteronomy 10:21

Jesus used so many miracles in His life to teach and preach. Jesus knew who and whose He was. He used His miracles for other people ... not for himself.

How has Jesus used a miracle in Your life for His glory? Share it here and then share it with someone today.

Quarter One

Quarter Two

Quarter Three

Quarter Four

Day
Sixty-seven

Matthew 17:20

Sometimes our faith is strong, and sometimes it is not.
Sometimes we must borrow faith from someone else,
or sometimes they have to borrow it from us.

Who can you borrow faith from today if you needed it?
And who can you share your faith
with today who might need it?

Quarter One

Quarter Two

Quarter Three

Quarter Four

Day
Sixty-eight

Exodus 20:4-6, Genesis 1:26-28

God created us, in His image, to live the life He called us to live. But far too often, we can find ourselves creating the life WE want to live. We are too busy making God in OUR image.

Are you living your life created in His image or yours? How can you tell the difference?

Quarter One

Quarter Two

Quarter Three

Quarter Four

Day
Sixty-nine

Ephesians 2:6

It is so funny how often people say, "I can't find Jesus in my life," or "I am not sure I even believe in Jesus," or "Jesus does not help me."

Jesus won't go where he is not wanted. He is always there; the question is, do we seek Him?

How are you seeking Jesus in your life?

How have you invited him to be a part of your day-to-day life?

Is Jesus welcomed?

Quarter One

_____

_____

_____

_____

Quarter Two

_____

_____

_____

_____

Quarter Three

_____

_____

_____

_____

Quarter Four

_____

_____

_____

_____

Day Seventy

Matthew 10: 38-39

Jesus calls us to take up our cross and follow Him. We are to die to ourselves and to follow Jesus above all others.

What are some opportunities where you can take ACTION to follow Jesus in your life?

Quarter One

Quarter Two

Quarter Three

Quarter Four

Day
Seventy-one

*Matthew 28: 19-20,
Acts 1:8*

We are called to be on mission for God. Seek and you shall find. Ask and it will be answered. Make known to others who Christ is in our lives. These are all asks of us from God. Are you really a Christian if no one ever finds out?

Does everyone in your life know you are a Christian? Why or why not? How are you showing others by your actions and your words?

Quarter One

Quarter Two

Quarter Three

Quarter Four

Day Seventy-two

Revelation 1:3

We are making investments in an eternal bank account every day. When we spend time in God's Word, we are making investments that are without measure.

How are you investing in your eternal bank account every day? How are you spending time in the Word?

Quarter One

Quarter Two

Quarter Three

Quarter Four

Day
Seventy-three

*Acts 1:4-8,
John 14: 25-26*

No one likes to be told no. Even when we were children, we did not like the word no. But when you listen and follow the NO of the Holy Spirit, it is then easier to follow the GO of the Holy Spirit.

Where is the Holy Spirit telling you no right now? And where is He telling you Go?

Quarter One

Quarter Two

Quarter Three

Quarter Four

Day
Seventy-four

Deuteronomy 30:15–16

Life is a series of choices.
Christ is the eternal fork in the road for all of us.

Where was your fork in the road?
How did you choose the Christ path?

Quarter One

Quarter Two

Quarter Three

Quarter Four

Day Seventy-five

Psalms 127: 28–29

Sometimes life seems out of control; we've all been there at times. Know this: Jesus is always carrying the moment, even when the moment is out of control.

Where does life seem out of control for you right now? Where do you need to relinquish control to Him?

Quarter One

_____
_____
_____
_____

Quarter Two

_____
_____
_____
_____

Quarter Three

_____
_____
_____
_____

Quarter Four

_____
_____
_____
_____

Day
Seventy-six

Genesis 1:1

God wrote your story from beginning to end.
He knows every single happening in your life.
Jesus wants to transform your life, guiding you toward
a future filled with abundance He has created for you.

Do you need your perspective changed? How does your story align with the abundant story He has written for you?

Quarter One

Quarter Two

Quarter Three

Quarter Four

Day
Seventy-seven

Luke 9:23

We are changed when we commit to following Jesus. We become His disciples. As a disciple is a follower of Jesus, we are on a mission with Jesus.

Are you a disciple of Jesus? How so?

Quarter One

Quarter Two

Quarter Three

Quarter Four

Day
Seventy-eight

Isaiah 59:2

Sin is spiritual cancer. It must not be allowed in our lives, and yet we all fall victim to it at times, for we are all sinners. We must pray for grace regarding our sins and ask for God's protection.

Where do you need grace and protection for your sins today?

Quarter One

Quarter Two

Quarter Three

Quarter Four

Day
Seventy-nine

Matthew 7:7

Have you ever wondered why God does not answer your prayers? What if the reason you do not have is because you have not asked God? For the Bible tells us, "Ask and you shall receive."

What are you asking God for today?

Quarter One

Quarter Two

Quarter Three

Quarter Four

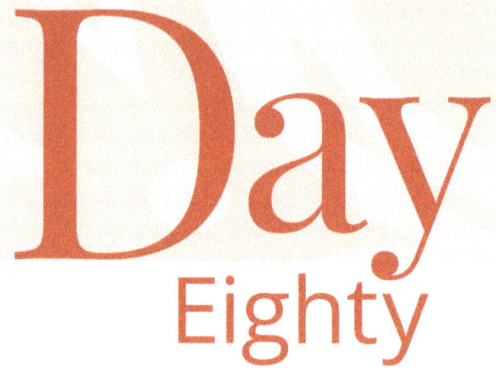

Day
Eighty

John 4:23

The gospel is an invitation for God to find favor in us rather than us finding favor in Him. HE SOUGHT US.

Where is God seeking you in your life? Is it in your work, your relationship, your parenting, your calling? Where is He seeking and calling you today?

Quarter One

Quarter Two

Quarter Three

Quarter Four

Day
Eighty-one

II Peter 1:21, Acts 27:17

What if we listened differently? What if we stopped listening to our heads and instead listened and were moved by the Holy Spirit?

What does that look like for you today?
How can you listen and be moved by the Holy Spirit?

Quarter One

Quarter Two

Quarter Three

Quarter Four

Day
Eighty-two

2 Timothy 3:16–17

All scripture is God-breathed. We use scripture for learning, teaching, and correcting to align with true righteousness. We must first spend time in the Word to understand what all of it means in our life.

How are you spending time understanding God's words? What stories have you told yourself as to why you are not spending time in God's words?

Quarter One

Quarter Two

Quarter Three

Quarter Four

Day Eighty-three

Ephesians 4:22–24

Sometimes life can get uncomfortable. Doing what is right in God's eyes is not always easy. God cares more about your character than He does your comfort.

What is something you know God is calling you to do that is uncomfortable?

Quarter One

___

Quarter Two

___

Quarter Three

___

Quarter Four

Day
Eighty-four

2 Corinthians 9:8–10

So many of us search for blessings in our lives.
We hunger as if we don't think we have, and we thirst for
things that seem to avoid us. All we want is the blessing,
but God says the blessings are already ours.
Are you missing the blessings God has already given you?

What blessings has God already given you?
Make a list of them today for this quarter.

Quarter One

Quarter Two

Quarter Three

Quarter Four

Day Eighty-five

I Corinthians 6:1–8

We live in a time where we judge so quickly. Where, in a moment, we can type a judgmental comment. It has become so easy, it happens far too often, and it is so damning. God calls us to be the defendant rather than the prosecutor.

Where in your life and to whom have you been the prosecutor and not the defendant? How can you make amends?

Quarter One

Quarter Two

Quarter Three

Quarter Four

Day
Eighty-six

Matthew 6:6

Have you ever thought about how and what you pray for?

There are three important components of our prayer life:
Pray to discern God's will in our lives.
Pray to do God's will in our lives.
Pray to display God's will in our lives.

Think about your daily prayers.
Where can I strengthen my prayer life?
Which of these prayers could I focus on for a time?
Is there one area of my prayer life I could use to strengthen?

Quarter One

Quarter Two

Quarter Three

Quarter Four

Day Eighty-seven

Matthew 5:12

The work we do for Jesus is never time wasted. No matter how little or futile it might seem in the moment, it is never wasted.

What work are you doing every day for Jesus? (Either paid work or not)

Quarter One

Quarter Two

Quarter Three

Quarter Four

Day
Eighty-eight

Psalms 46:10,
Psalms 46: 1-3

They say it is through difficult times that we are most tested in our faith. God uses difficult times in our lives to teach us to pray, mold our faith, and grow closer to Him.

How has God used a difficult time this quarter to draw you closer to Him?

Quarter One

Quarter Two

Quarter Three

Quarter Four

Day
Eighty-nine

Isaiah 1:17

We all seem to have a cause now. We all seem to have a platform. But be careful about fighting for Jesus just for the sake of fighting.

Do you find yourself fighting just for the sake of fighting? Write those areas down, and ask God for His guidance and direction to let go and direct your steps to His calling for you.

Quarter One

Quarter Two

Quarter Three

Quarter Four

Day Ninety

Acts 1:8

We are not judges. We are not prosecutors. We are called witnesses only. All the time, in every circumstance.

Where are you the judge in your life rather than the witness?

Quarter One

Quarter Two

Quarter Three

Quarter Four

Day
Ninety-one

James 1:5–8

Do you ever wonder why what we "want" does not seem to happen? What if God waits on us to ask before doing something?

What would you ask God for today? How would your prayers be different now?

Quarter One

Quarter Two

Quarter Three

Quarter Four

Day
Ninety-two

Thessalonians 5:16, John 14:13–14

No matter what, Pray. No matter when, Pray. No matter who, Pray. Prayers should never be your last resort; they should come first.

When do you find yourself praying? How can you change that?

Quarter One

Quarter Two

Quarter Three

Quarter Four

Quarter 1
Action Plan

As you embark on this new quarter, take a moment to reflect on the previous months by reviewing your journal entries. Note the Bible verses that resonated with you, the key questions and insights that emerged, and the actions you are inspired to take to deepen your faith and draw closer to God. Use the provided action plan pages to document your spiritual journey, identifying areas of growth and recognizing opportunities for further improvement. This practice will help you to continuously nurture your faith and strengthen your walk with God.

Action Plan

Action Plan

Quarter 2
Action Plan

As you embark on this new quarter, take a moment to reflect on the previous months by reviewing your journal entries. Note the Bible verses that resonated with you, the key questions and insights that emerged, and the actions you are inspired to take to deepen your faith and draw closer to God. Use the provided action plan pages to document your spiritual journey, identifying areas of growth and recognizing opportunities for further improvement. This practice will help you to continuously nurture your faith and strengthen your walk with God.

Action Plan

Action Plan

Quarter 3
Action Plan

As you embark on this new quarter, take a moment to reflect on the previous months by reviewing your journal entries. Note the Bible verses that resonated with you, the key questions and insights that emerged, and the actions you are inspired to take to deepen your faith and draw closer to God. Use the provided action plan pages to document your spiritual journey, identifying areas of growth and recognizing opportunities for further improvement. This practice will help you to continuously nurture your faith and strengthen your walk with God.

Action Plan

Action Plan

Quarter 4
Action Plan

As you embark on this new quarter, take a moment to reflect on the previous months by reviewing your journal entries. Note the Bible verses that resonated with you, the key questions and insights that emerged, and the actions you are inspired to take to deepen your faith and draw closer to God. Use the provided action plan pages to document your spiritual journey, identifying areas of growth and recognizing opportunities for further improvement. This practice will help you to continuously nurture your faith and strengthen your walk with God.

Action Plan

Action Plan

About the Author

Cathy Tooley is a passionate educator, speaker, and faith-driven leader with more than thirty years of experience in K–12 education. A former high school English and Spanish teacher turned administrator, Cathy has dedicated her life to empowering educators and shaping future leaders with compassion, wisdom, and grace.

She is the founder and CEO of Tools for Success, an organization committed to closing systemic gaps in education through support, training, and encouragement. Cathy's first book, *The Education System Is Broken: Strategies to Rebuilding Hope, Lives, and Futures*, reflects her heart for renewal and transformation—values that also guide her walk with Christ.

Grounded in her faith and driven by purpose, Cathy now shares her love for God and personal growth through this devotional journal. Her hope is to inspire women to embrace each day with intention, courage, and the confidence that comes from knowing they are deeply loved by their Creator.

www.ingramcontent.com/pod-product-compliance
Lightning Source LLC
Chambersburg PA
CBHW040315170426
43196CB00020B/2924